Welcome to the world of ocean animals!

Which ocean animals do you know? Would you like to make some of your own and find out loads of fun facts about them along the way? Then this book is for you!

Follow the easy step by step instructions to start creating your own ocean animal collection. When you have finished making a creature, you can also think about where it might live – on the seabed or by the shore.

A lot of the projects use paint and PVA glue. When you use either of them, always cover surfaces with a piece of plastic or layers of old newspaper. Whenever you can, leave the project to dry before moving on to the next step. This avoids things getting stuck to each other or paint smudging.

So, do you have your craft tools at the ready? Then get set to make your crafty creatures and discover what makes each of them so special!

PINK FOAM SHRIMP

You will need:
Pink foam
Pink pipe cleaners
Double sided tape
Black marker pen
Scissors
Stapler
Ruler

There are many different kinds of shrimp. A lot of them live in the depths of the ocean. They swim up to the water's surface to feed on tiny plants.

1

Using the black marker pen, draw some shapes on the pink foam: a heart shape, 5 circles and a tail shape.

2

Cut out each of the shapes using the scissors. Make sure you cut inside the line to remove the black lines of the marker pen.

3

Cut out a pink foam square that is 10 x 10cm. Staple it together to form a cylinder. Next, cut out a small rectangle of pink foam and cut slits into one short edge.

4

Use the double sided tape to stick the circles onto the cylinder. Next, tape the heart-shaped head and the tail on. Press the back end of the cylinder to flatten it.

5

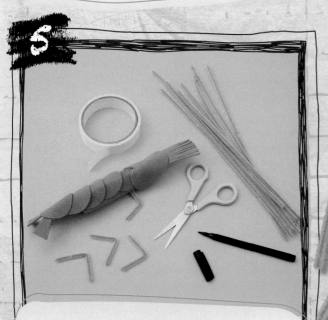

Stick the frayed foam to the front of the head. Cut pipe cleaners to form legs and feelers. Attach them by poking them through the foam. Draw on eyes.

SHRIMP FACT

All kinds of shrimp live in large groups, called colonies. Some colonies are made up of about 350 shrimps!

BALLOON WHALE

Blue whales are the largest animals that have ever lived on our planet. They are 30 metres long, and their tongues can weigh as much as an elephant!

1

Cut out a circle from the dark blue card that has a 10cm diameter. Stuff the balloon with the toy filling and stick on the googly eye.

2

Cut 2 strips of dark blue card that are 30cm long and 1 strip of white card that is the same length. Cut one long edge of each strip so that it looks like waves. You can use special scissors for this if you like.

3

Layer the strips with the white one in the middle. Bend them and staple them together to form a ring. Stick this onto the blue circle with tape.

4

Cut out a rectangle from the dark blue card. Fold the rectangle to make a box and stick it down in the centre of the circle.

5

Cut a tail out of the light blue card and attach it to your whale with sticky tape. Use the pen to draw the whale's mouth. Then glue the whale onto the box.

WHALE FACT
A blue whale's heart is the same size as a small car!

7

SANDPAPER STARFISH

You will need:
Sandpaper
Crayons
Pencil
Ruler
Scissors

Starfish live at the bottom of oceans. You can sometimes find them in rock pools, too. You can make these starfish and keep them anywhere in your home!

1

Use the crayons to draw small circles all over the rough sandpaper. The circles should look like scales.

2

Turn the sandpaper over. Draw a 5-point star shape onto the smooth back using the ruler and pencil.

3

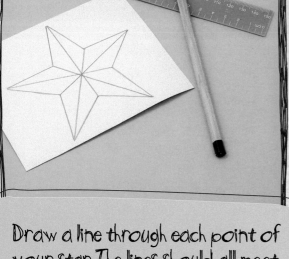

Draw a line through each point of your star. The lines should all meet in the centre of the star. Cut your star out using the scissors.

4

Round off each point of the star, using the scissors.

5

Fold the starfish along each line and then pinch each point. The points form the arms of your starfish.

STARFISH FACT
If a starfish loses one of its arms, it can grow a new one!

TISSUE PAPER CORAL REEF

You will need:
Tissue paper
Paper cup
Double sided tape
Wool
Glue stick
Yellow card
Scissors
Sticky tape
Pencil

Coral reefs are like big underwater landscapes. They are home to thousands of different kinds of ocean animals.

1

Cut a curved shape out of the yellow card. Cover the cup in a layer of double sided tape. Remove the tape's back and wrap the wool around the cup until it is covered.

2

Take 2 sheets of tissue paper and start rolling each of them up into a tube shape. Cut a fringe into the edge of each of them.

3

Flatten each tube and roll it up. Secure it in place with double sided tape. Make lots of these corals using different coloured tissue paper.

4

Scrunch up some sheets of tissue paper into long thin sticks. Stand some in the paper cup. Tape others together into a bunch.

5

Glue all the tissue paper coral onto the yellow card. Fill the gaps by scrunching up tissue paper into balls and sticking them on, too.

CORAL REEF FACT
The world's biggest coral reef is the Great Barrier Reef by Australia. It is 8,000 years old!

PAPER PLATE SEAHORSES

You will need:
Paper plate
Tissue paper
Glue stick
Black felt tipped pen
Scissors
Googly eyes

Seahorses often swim in pairs, linked together by their tails. You can make two seahorses from the one paper plate, so that you can link yours, too!

1

2

Draw a seahorse shape along the edge of your paper plate. Cut this out with scissors.

Trace around this shape on the other side of the plate. Cut this seahorse out, too.

3

Cover your seahorses with strips of tissue paper. If the strips are too long, fold them around the edge of the seahorses.

4

Cut a fin for each seahorse out of the paper plate. Cover them in tissue paper and stick them on.

5

Draw around each seahorse with the felt tipped pen. Glue a googly eye to the head of each seahorse.

SEAHORSE FACT
Seahorses can move each of their eyes on its own, so they can look in two directions at the same time!

HERMIT CRAB

Hermit crabs live in shells that they find on the ocean floor. They carry their shell with them wherever they go. Give your crab a home that stands out from the crowd!

You will need:
Small paper plate
Orange pom poms
(1 large, 2 small)
Orange pipe cleaners
Double sided tape
Sequins
Scissors
Orange foam
Stapler
PVA glue
Googly eyes

1

Stick a layer of double sided tape along the rim of the paper plate. Take off the back of the tape and scatter some sequins on top. Shake off any loose sequins.

2

Cut through the centre of the plate, but stop short of cutting it in half. Curl the plate into a shell shape and secure it in place with a staple.

3

Twist 4 pipe cleaners together in the middle and spread them out to form a star shape.

4

Cut out 6 cone shapes from orange foam. Stick some double sided tape onto one side, remove the back and wrap each cone around a pipe cleaner.

5

Curl the ends of the remaining 2 pipe cleaners and stick the googly eyes onto them. Tape the pipe cleaners to the inside of the shell. Glue the pom poms behind the eyes.

HERMIT CRAB FACT

A hermit crab's shell is not just its home. It also protects the crab's body, which is very soft.

15

PAPER MACHE TURTLE

Sea turtles are great swimmers. They use their strong flippers to push themselves through the water. A turtle can swim non-stop for weeks at a time!

You will need:
2 small bowls
Green and brown tissue paper
Cling film
PVA glue
Water
Paint brush
Green card
Dark green paint
Black felt tipped pen
Scissors

1

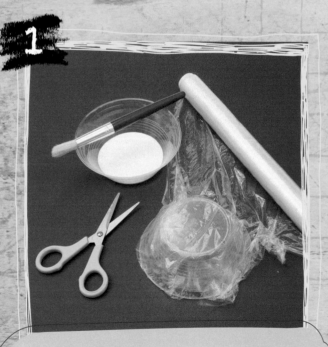

Cover one of the bowls in cling film. Use the other bowl to mix some water with the same amount of PVA glue.

2

Cover the bowl in pieces of brown and green tissue paper, sticking them in place with the PVA glue mix. Make sure you have at least 3 layers of tissue paper. Leave to dry.

3

Scrunch up tissue paper. Dip it into green paint to print a pattern on the green card.

4

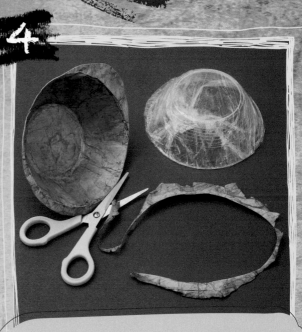

Carefully remove the tissue paper shell from the bowl. Trim the edges using the scissors.

5

Cut a head, tail and 4 flippers out of the printed card. Stick them to the underside of the shell using sticky tape.

TURTLE FACT
Sea turtles can weigh over 900 kilograms. That's about as much as a small car!

WOOLLY JUMPER SHARK

Did you know that sharks have many rows of teeth? They lose so many teeth in their lifetime that they need to grow thousands of new ones!

1

Cut the sleeve off an old jumper. The sleeve should be 30cm long. Turn it inside out and tie the cut end together with embroidery thread.

2

Turn the sleeve back the right way and fill it with the toy stuffing. Fold the cuff in on itself and glue it in place to make the mouth.

18

3

Cover the opening in your shark's mouth with a scrap piece of the jumper. Cut out 2 rows of white teeth from the foam. Glue them into the mouth.

4

Cut out fins and a tail from the blue foam. Glue them onto your shark's body.

5

Glue on the googly eyes to finish.

SHARK FACT

Did you know that sharks have a great sense of smell? People sometimes call them 'swimming noses'!

PLASTIC BAG JELLYFISH

You will need:
Large plastic sandwich bags
White pipe cleaners
Pastel-coloured gift ribbon
Sticky tape
Scissors
Ruler

Jellyfish come in many different shapes and sizes. Some can be as big as a human! You can make yours to be as big or small as you like.

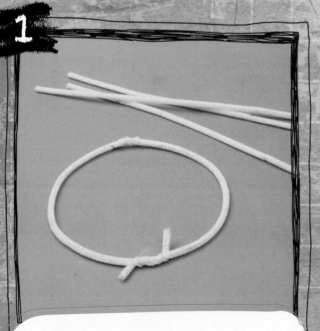

1 Twist the ends of 2 pipe cleaners together and bend them to form a circle.

2 Cut off long strands of the gift ribbon. Curl the ends by firmly running them over the edge of a ruler.

20

3

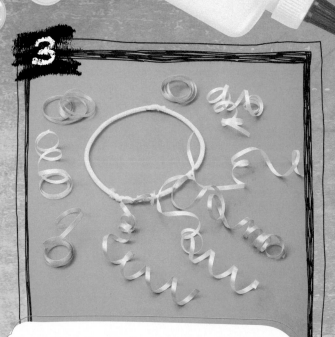

Tie the curled ribbon strands to the pipe cleaner ring.

4

Tie a knot into each sealed corner of the plastic bag. Turn the bag inside out and stick its open side to the ring.

5

Cut out long strips of plastic from the other bags. Stick their ends to the knots inside the one forming your jellyfish. Stick a short loop of plastic to the top so that you can hang up your jellyfish.

JELLYFISH FACT

Did you know that jellyfish have lived on Earth for millions of years?

CLOWNFISH HOME

Clownfish have a very special home: they live in the tentacles of creatures called sea anemones. You can make your very own clownfish in its home!

1

Cut the bubble wrap and tissue paper in half, lengthways. Glue them together along one long edge. Cut a fringe down the other edge.

2

Roll up the tissue paper/bubblewrap strips into tubes. Fix these in place with sticky tape. Repeat this with the other tissue paper sheets. Stick all the tubes onto the yellow card.

3

Press the polystyrene egg onto the wooden skewer. Paint on thick orange stripes. Leave to dry.

4

Cut out fins and a tail from the orange card. Stick them onto the body of your clownfish.

5

Use the marker pen to draw the details onto your fish. Glue on googly eyes. Stick the wooden skewer into one of the anemones.

CLOWNFISH FACT

Clownfish come in all sorts of colours, such as yellow, red, black, dark blue and white.

GLOSSARY

pair	a set of two things, people or animals
rock pool	pools of seawater on rocky beaches
scales	the thin, overlapping parts that make up the skin of a fish or a snake
tentacles	long thin parts of an animal's body; the animal uses its tentacles to feel and hold things

INDEX

Published in paperback in 2017 by Wayland

Copyright © Hodder and Stoughton, 2017

Wayland, an imprint of Hachette Children's Group
Part of Hodder and Stoughton

Carmelite House
50 Victoria Embankment
London, EC4Y 0DZ

All rights reserved.

An Hachette UK Company
www.hachette.co.uk www.hachettechildrens.co.uk

Series editor: Julia Adams
Craft photography: Simon Pask, N1 Studios
Additional images: Shutterstock

Dewey classification: 745.5-dc23
ISBN: 9780750297202
ebook ISBN: 9780750295659

Printed in China

The QR codes included in this book were valid at the time of going to press. However, because of the nature of the Internet, it is possible that addresses may have changed, or sites may have changed or closed down, since publication.

FSC
www.fsc.org

MIX
Paper from
responsible sources
FSC® C104740